Read & Respond

FOR KS2

Read & Respond

FOR KS2

Author: Gillian Howell

Development Editor: Alex Albrighton

Assistant Editors: Roanne Charles and Pam Kelt

Series Designer: Anna Oliwa

Designer: Liz Gilbert

Illustrations: Nick Sharratt

Text © 2010 Gillian Howell   © 2010 Scholastic Ltd

Designed using Adobe InDesign

Published by Scholastic Ltd.
Book End, Range Road, Witney,
Oxfordshire OX29 0YD
www.scholastic.co.uk

Printed by Bell & Bain

1 2 3 4 5 6 7 8 9   0 1 2 3 4 5 6 7 8 9

British Library Cataloguing-in-Publication Data
A catalogue record for this book is available from the
British Library.

ISBN 978-1407-11366-1

Acknowledgements

The publishers gratefully acknowledge permission to reproduce the following copyright material: **David Higham Associates** for the use of text extracts and illustrations from *Cliffhanger* by Jacqueline Wilson text © 1995, Jacqueline Wilson, illustrations © 1995, Nick Sharratt (1995, Corgi Yearling). Every effort has been made to trace copyright holders for the works reproduced in this book, and the publishers apologise for any inadvertent omissions.

Cliffhanger

About the book

Cliffhanger is a story about a boy called Tim and his experiences on an adventure holiday. Written in the first person, the book instantly appeals to readers as they are easily able to empathise with Tim and his fears and concerns. It is written in six short chapters, each one preceded by a postcard home written by Tim. This also tells readers about how Tim is feeling and gives a clue about what might happen in the next chapter. *Cliffhanger* was originally written as a two-part television drama script for the Channel 4 Schools series *Talk, Write and Read* in 1995.

Tim hates sports of all kinds and is rather shy and self-conscious. However, his dad is very sporty and thinks an adventure holiday will toughen Tim up, so he is forced to go. Tim's mum is worried about him and promises to collect him if he really hates it. She asks him to send lots of postcards.

Things go wrong from the very beginning when Tim leaves his beloved teddy, Walter Bear, behind. At the Adventure Centre, all the children are arranged into teams: Lions, Panthers, Cheetahs and Tigers. Tim is put into Tigers and shares a room with two other boys in the same team – the very snobbish and sporty Giles, and another sport-hating boy called Biscuits, who is obsessed with food. Giles makes fun of both boys, but Tim and Biscuits become friends.

The first activity is a game called Triangles and Tim finds he is hopeless at it. In fact, no one else is as hopeless as he is, so he sends the first postcard home, pleading to be collected.

The next day's activity is abseiling. Tim forgets to obey the main rule: *Don't let go of the rope!* and ends up dangling halfway down the cliff.

The final activity is an obstacle race where the children have to carry buckets of water and fill a container situated across a stream. No one succeeds until Tim uses his brain to work out a strategy and his team are declared the winners. Tim is now a hero and is enjoying himself so much he doesn't want the holiday to end.

About the author

Jacqueline Wilson was born in Bath in 1945 and grew up in Kingston-on-Thames, where she still lives today. She has written many books for children, and her sensitive understanding of the way children live and the problems they encounter, together with her sense of humour, have made her an extremely popular author. She has sold millions of books – her total stands at more than 20 million in the UK alone. In June 2002 Jacqueline was given an OBE for services to literacy in schools and was made a Dame in the New Year's Honours List for 2008. She was Children's Laureate from 2005 to 2007.

> **Facts and figures**
> Jacqueline Wilson's work has been on countless shortlists and has won many awards, including the Smarties Prize and the Children's Book Award. *The Illustrated Mum* won the Guardian Children's Fiction Award and the 1999 Children's Book of the Year at the British Book Awards. It was also shortlisted for the 1999 Whitbread Children's Book Award. *The Story of Tracy Beaker* won the 2002 Blue Peter People's Choice Award.

Guided reading

Introducing the book

Show the front cover to the children and read the title of the book. Ask the children if any of them already know anything about this story and who wrote it. Invite them to find and read the name of the author. Have they read any other books written by Jacqueline Wilson? Write a list of any titles the children have read.

Discuss the type of stories they are and ask the children to compare any similarities or differences in the styles and themes of the stories.

If any of the children have already read this book, explain that reading it again in a group will help them to explore the story in greater detail, but ask them not to spoil the plot for other readers as you go through each of the chapters.

Turn to the back cover and read the blurb. Ask the children to suggest how they think Tim will cope with the various activities on the adventure holiday.

Read the introduction from the author before the children begin reading the story.

Chapters One and Two

In the opening chapter, readers are immediately introduced to Tim and his parents. The difference between his mum's and dad's characters is established and so is Tim's relationship with each of them.

The chapter begins with Tim setting the background to being sent on the holiday and describes the journey and the first day at the centre. The other main characters – Kelly, Giles and Biscuits – are introduced.

Identify any vocabulary that might be challenging before the children begin to read – for example, *abseiling*, *privately* and *wrestling*. Remind the children to use their knowledge of phonics and syllables to segment and blend any words they are unsure about.

Ask the children to read the first page and to describe their initial impressions about the personalities of Dad, Mum and Tim. Encourage them to describe how Tim's relationship with his mother is different from his relationship with his father. Ask the children to read up to *Oh oh! Swopsies*. Ask them how the character of Kelly is introduced to the story. What sort of personality does Kelly have? Ask each child to suggest an adjective that could be used to describe her. Do the children think that Tim and Kelly will be friends in the story? Ask them to give a reason for their opinion.

Encourage the children to describe their initial feelings about the characters of Giles and Biscuits. Do they think either of them will become friends with Tim or with each other? Ask them to give a reason.

At the end of Chapter One, invite the children to describe how they think Tim is feeling and why. How would they feel if they were in Tim's situation?

In Chapter Two, Tim begins to enjoy his friendship with Biscuits and Kelly and thinks he might actually enjoy the adventure holiday – apart from the activities, that is. But the first activity, a game called Triangles, confirms his fears that he will indeed hate it. He pleads in vain with his parents to collect him.

Ask the children to continue reading to the end of Chapter Two. Encourage them to read the words in italic print with expression. Ask them to explain why Tim comments: *But you can't always trust your parents.* (Tim's mum had promised to collect him but fails to keep her promise.)

When the children have finished the chapter, ask them to describe what they think is good about Tim's experience and what is bad. Invite them to support their ideas by finding examples in the text.

Encourage the children to say why they think the author added that Giles and Biscuits had brought cuddly toys to the centre. (To emphasise how sad Tim feels without Walter Bear.) Invite the class to predict what will happen to Tim during abseiling.

Chapters Three and Four

Tim is forced to abseil down a cliff. Because he is so frightened about it, he doesn't really listen to the team leader's instructions so he forgets to

Guided reading

hold on to the rope and ends up dangling halfway down, terrified. Even when he regains control and reaches the bottom, he says, *Never ever ever again!* The team leader, Jake, tries to boost Tim's confidence at the end of the chapter by saying he is amazing at working things out.

Chapter Four features a canoeing race, which Tim and Biscuits don't take very seriously, and Tim is enjoying himself. The Tigers are winning the race when Kelly drops her troll doll into the river. Tim and Biscuits go to the rescue, much to Giles' horror as this means the Tigers come last. However, Kelly now thinks Tim is a hero.

Before you begin reading these chapters, find the hyphenated word *tri-umphantly* near the beginning of Chapter Four and point it out to the children. Ask the children to read the word syllable by syllable. Is the word usually spelled with a hyphen? Why is it hyphenated here? (It is too long for the end of the line of print.) Turn to the section of Chapter Five where Kelly pushes over a Cheetah and ask the children to scan the page and find the word again.

Point out the chant *Dan-de-dan-dan-daaan* halfway through Chapter Four and remind the children to use the italic print to give expression to their reading.

Now invite the children to read Chapter Three, beginning with the postcard and, when they have finished, to describe how Tim really feels about the experience.

Ask them how the postcard helps to add humour to Tim's situation. Talk about how Jake helps Tim in this chapter. Did Jake really need Tim to help him find the lost balls? What was his motive in asking Tim? (To get Tim on his own and try to boost his confidence.) Do they children think Jake's chat at the end of the chapter will work? Encourage them to say why or why not.

Ask the children to continue reading to the end of Chapter Four. When they have finished, invite them to describe in their own words how Giles treats Tim in both chapters.

They should also compare Giles' bullying with the behaviour of the others in their team.

You might like to spend a few moments talking with the group about bullying, what Tim should do to cope with Giles and what they would do in a similar situation. Ask them if they think Tim will continue to hate the adventure camp now that he has had some fun with his new friends.

Chapters Five and Six

Here, the final activity of the holiday takes place. The Crazy Bucket race is run over an obstacle course with the team members carrying buckets of water. Jake and Sally explain the rules, while Tim and Biscuits groan about how much running is involved.

In the final element of the race, Tim is the only one who uses his brain to solve the puzzle of how to pour the buckets of water into the 'baby big cat' containers, making his team the winners. Tim is now their hero.

In Chapter Six, Tim is enjoying the holiday so much that he almost wishes it would last longer. The Tigers are the overall winners and each member gets a soft-toy tiger.

On the final night, Tim goes to sleep cuddling his new toy and no longer misses Walter Bear. The story finishes with two postcards – one from Tim to Kelly and one from Tim to Biscuits.

Before asking the children to read the last two chapters, ask the children to find the word *whimsy*, near the beginning of Chapter Five. Invite them to suggest what the word means and if necessary, use a dictionary to find out. Ask them to read the postcard at the beginning of the chapter and to say how the tone of Tim's writing has changed from the postcards in the first few chapters.

Now invite the children to read Chapter Five. When they have finished, ask them to describe how Tim feels about the bucket race at the beginning of the chapter. To support their answer, ask them to find something that Tim says. Can they locate the point in the chapter where Tim begins to feel more confident about his chances of succeeding? (When he realises he can go slowly.)

Guided reading

Later in the chapter, ask the children why they think Jake asks Tim if he has any ideas for how to get the water across the stream. (In Chapter Three, Jake had said Tim was good at sussing things out.)

Discuss how Tim finally stands up to Giles and find the evidence in the text. Why do they think Tim didn't stand up for himself sooner? What made Tim choose this moment to confront Giles? Then invite the children to describe how the Tigers filled up their containers. Ask them to describe how the chapter ends and to consider how Tim might be feeling now.

Before they read the final chapter, ask the children to predict how the story will end. Look at the first paragraph and point out the way *t-i-c-k* is written. Ask the children to suggest how they should read these words.

Remind them to use the different ways that words are written to help them use an expressive tone. Invite them to read to the end of the story and compare their predictions with the story ending.

Discuss the story as a whole. Invite the children to say what the story is about and to suggest what the main theme of the story is. Ask the children to say if they enjoyed the story and give reasons why or why not. Finally, see if they can suggest what further adventures Tim, Biscuits and Kelly could have together.

Shared reading

Extract 1

● Recap how Tim has been sent, against his will, on an adventure holiday, up to the point where Giles is showing off his tennis racket.

● Encourage the children to read the extract aloud with you. Invite them to identify the spoken words and highlight the speech punctuation. Underline the words *squeaked* and *jeered*. Ask the children to read the spoken words where these speech verbs have been used instead of *said* with appropriate expression. Challenge the children to identify two other examples of

how the author has indicated the way the words should be spoken. (*said Giles scornfully* and *said Biscuits, grinning.*) Ask them to suggest how to turn the adverb *scornfully* into a speech verb (*scorned*). How could they use *grinning* as a speech verb?

● Talk about how Tim is feeling in this extract. Ask the children if Jacqueline Wilson tells the reader directly or gives clues. Invite them to find and highlight the author's words that indicate Tim's emotions.

Extract 2

● This extract is from Chapter Three, when the children go abseiling.

● Recap the preceding dialogue, explaining how the author has used short sentences of alternate dialogue to build tension.

● Remind the children of the conventions for setting out dialogue. Point out how a new speaker begins on a new line. Invite the children to highlight the speech punctuation.

● Now read the extract out loud, up to *Start backing towards the edge*. Point out how Tim's thoughts are described in longer sentences here.

Ask the children what effect this has on the reader. (It slows down the pace slightly.)

● Now invite the children to read to the end of the extract. Encourage them to identify the short and incomplete sentences and to describe the effect this style has on the way they read. Ask: *What does the 'dot, dot, dot' (ellipsis) suggest?*

● Ask the children to underline the use of italic print in the extract. (*don't*, *Help!* and *I let go of the rope!*) Invite them to re-read the lines with italics using expressive voices.

Extract 3

● This extract comes from Chapter Five and describes the final activity of the holiday.

● Before reading the extract with the children, discuss what has just happened. (One of the Cheetahs has bumped into Tim, knocking him over.) Mask the last lines from after *You can't let us down, Tim*. Highlight the words *sprawling* and *spurted*. Invite the children to say what they think the words mean and to suggest alternative words.

● Invite the children to read the text with you. Ask them to suggest what Tim is thinking when

he looks first at Biscuits, then at Kelly, and Laura and Lesley. What might he be thinking when he looks at Giles?

● Encourage the children to explain their answers, then ask them to talk with a partner for a few moments about what they think Tim will do next.

● Reveal the last lines and read the remainder of the extract together. Read the last two sentences to the class again, adding *so* between the sentences. Ask them to say which version is most effective at showing how Tim feels at this point.

Extract 1

Me

Chapter One

I started unpacking all my stuff. My T-shirts and pyjamas smelt all clean and flowery of home. I had to bend over my bag so that Giles and Biscuits wouldn't see my watery eyes.

Then I felt a sudden bang on the head.

'Watch out!' I squeaked.

'Sorry. Just practising,' said Giles. 'Oh goodness, you're not blubbing, are you? I hardly touched you.'

I sniffed hard.

'Have you brought your tennis racquet then?' Giles asked.

I started to worry some more.

'I thought they were meant to provide all the racquets and that,' I said.

'That's right,' said Biscuits. He quietly passed me a tissue. It was a bit chocolatey but it was still fine for mopping operations.

'It'll be just ropey old stuff,' said Giles scornfully. 'I've brought my own equipment.'

He started rifling through his bags, showing us. It all looked brand new and very expensive.

'I've brought my own equipment too,' said Biscuits, grinning. He nudged me and pulled open a big picnic bag. I saw bags and bags of biscuits, crisps, apples, sweets and cans of cola.

'Yummy,' I said.

Biscuits rubbed his tummy.

Giles sighed in a superior manner.

'I've brought one bit of equipment,' I said, showing him my safety helmet.

I knew it was a mistake as soon as I'd got it out. Especially as Mum had painted TIM in bright pink letters on the front.

Text © 1995, Jacqueline Wilson; illustration © 1995, Nick Sharratt

READ & RESPOND: Activities based on *Cliffhanger*

SECTION
3

Extract 2

Chapter Three

'We all get scared,' said Jake. 'Especially the first time.' He bent down and looked me straight in the eye. 'But you'll see it's easy, Tim. Trust me. Now. Into the harness.'

I found I was being strapped in before I could get away. Jake was telling me things about this rope in this hand, that rope in that, but the wind was whipping his words away. I couldn't listen properly anyway. There was just this roaring inside my head.

'Don't let go of the rope, right?' said Jake.

I felt as if my head was going to burst right out of my personalized safety helmet.

This couldn't be real. It couldn't be happening to me. If I closed my eyes maybe it would all turn into a nightmare and then I'd wake up in bed at home with Walter Bear.

'Tim?' said Jake. 'Open your eyes! Now, your pal Biscuits is down there waiting for you. Come on. Start backing towards the edge.'

I backed one step. Then another. Then I stopped.

'I can't!'

'Yes you can,' said Jake. 'You'll see. Over you go. Don't worry. You can't fall. You just have to remember, you *don't* let go of the rope.'

I stared at him and started backing some more. Then my heels suddenly lost contact with the ground. I slipped backwards and suddenly ... there I was! Suspended. In mid-air.

'*Help!*'

I reached forward, desperate.

I had to hang on to something.

I grabbed at the rock.

I let go of the rope!

Text © 1995, Jacqueline Wilson; illustration © 1995, Nick Sharratt

Extract 3

Chapter Five

'You cheaty old Cheetah!' I heard Kelly bellow.

There was a yell and a thump and a splash. When I opened my eyes I saw the Cheetah sprawling on the ground, soaking wet, Kelly standing over him triumphantly.

'Hey! Hey! You'll all end up disqualified if you're not careful!' Jake called. 'Is Tim OK?'

I wasn't sure. There was wet on my knees. It wasn't just the water from my bucket. I was *bleeding*.

'Maybe you'd better go and get them bandaged?' said Biscuits.

I stood up very slowly. The blood spurted a bit more. I had a truly great excuse to get out of finishing the race.

I looked at Biscuits. I looked at Kelly. I looked at Laura and Lesley, who were running back to see if I was all right. I looked at Giles. He was yelling again.

'Come *on*! We've all got to finish. You can't let us down, Tim!'

I didn't mind letting Giles down *at all*. But I didn't want to spoil it for the others.

'I'm OK,' I said. 'I'll run back to fill my bucket again.'

'We'll wait for you,' said Biscuits.

'No, I'll catch you up.'

So I ran all the way back to the pool, even though my knees were hurting quite badly. Then I filled my bucket and started the long run again, way way way behind all the others, though two Lions then bumped into each other and had to go back to the pool as well. And more came a cropper on the slide. There was a whole bunch who fought to go first and spilled all their water. By the time *I* got to the slide it was clear and I could take it slowly. I didn't spill a drop.

Plot, character and setting

Scary moments

> **Objective:** To empathise with characters.
> **What you need:** Copies of *Cliffhanger* and copies of photocopiable page 15.
> **Cross-curricular links:** PSHE, citizenship.

What to do

● Use this activity after reading Chapter Three. Discuss how Tim feels during the chapter. Ask the children to describe activities that scare them. Ask them to describe their feelings when they are scared. Look through the chapter for words and phrases that show how Tim feels – for example, *started shaking*, and *roaring inside my head*.

● Ask the children to say what they do to help them when they feel scared. Together, draw up a list of words and phrases that describe their feelings from just beginning to get scared until they are feeling safe and secure again.

● Hand out copies of photocopiable page 15. Ask the children, in pairs, to add words and phrases to the timeline to describe how they feel and react when do something that scares them.

● When they have finished, invite some of the pairs to hold up their photocopiable sheets and describe the feelings they have listed. Compare their answers and look at how similar or different their choices are. Talk about whether and/or how the feelings build up to a climax. Discuss the words and phrases they chose to describe how they felt when the activity was over.

> **Differentiation**
> **For older/more confident learners:** Ask the children to write a complete sentence for each stage of the timeline using the first-person voice.
> **For younger/less confident learners:** Encourage the children to imagine they are abseiling for the first time and feel scared like Tim in the story. Ask them to write their feelings and reactions on the timeline.

Giles

> **Objective:** To empathise with characters.
> **What you need:** Copies of *Cliffhanger*.
> **Cross-curricular links:** PSHE, citizenship.

What to do

● When the children have completed reading the story, ask them to say from whose point of view the story is told. (Tim's.) Encourage the children to think about the character of Giles and invite them quickly to give you three words that describe him. Can they explain why they chose those words? Invite them to say how the author gives readers an impression of Giles' character. (Through his actions as seen by Tim, things he says and how he says them.)

● Ask the children to work with a partner and look through the text to find the parts of the story that feature Giles. Encourage them to find examples, not only when Giles is being critical of Tim and Biscuits, but also when Giles joins in with the others. Ask them to look for good points and bad points. Explain that they should make notes of words from the text and their own knowledge that would be useful for writing a character sketch.

● In a plenary, invite the children to give an oral description of Giles. Discuss whether they think Giles really is an unpleasant character and ask the children to make suggestions to explain why he behaves as he does.

> **Differentiation**
> **For older/more confident learners:** Let children do the activity individually, rather than in pairs.
> **For younger/less confident learners:** Children can work in a group with a supporting adult. Provide the group with a large sheet of paper with a line down the middle. Label one side *Good points* and the other *Bad points*. The supporting adult can scribe their suggestions on the sheet.

Plot, character and setting

Biscuits

> **Objective:** To empathise with characters.
> **What you need:** Copies of *Cliffhanger* and copies of photocopiable page 16.
> **Cross-curricular links:** PSHE, citizenship.

What to do

● This activity works best when the children have completed reading the book.

● Ask the children to find where Biscuits is introduced. (Near the end of Chapter One.) Invite them to say what they think Tim's first impression is of Biscuits and to find evidence in the text to support their ideas. (He added a P.S. to the postcard saying that Biscuits was a friend.) Ask the children to describe what Biscuits does and says in Chapter One that make Tim think he is a friend.

● Now invite them to look through the story with a partner to find the events that feature Biscuits.

Ask them to tell each other how they feel about what Biscuits does or says, then complete the photocopiable sheet by writing a word to describe Biscuits for each example from the text.

● In a plenary session, invite the children to share and compare the words they chose to describe Biscuits. If it turns out that many have chosen the same words, encourage them to use a thesaurus to find alternative examples. Finally, ask the children to summarise Biscuits' character orally in one sentence.

> **Differentiation**
> **For older/more confident learners:** Ask children to write a complete sentence to describe each example of Biscuits' speech or actions using their own adjectives.
> **For younger/less confident learners:** In a group, discuss Biscuit's character, then draw up a list of adjectives for the children to choose from before they complete the photocopiable sheet.

Viewpoint

> **Objective:** To take account of viewpoint, explaining how characters might see events from different points of view.
> **What you need:** Copies of *Cliffhanger* and character name cards for Giles, Biscuits, Kelly and Jake.

What to do

● When the children have read Chapter Three, ask them to say again from whose point of view the story is told. (Tim's.) Together, draw up a list of the other main characters in the chapter: Jake, Giles, Biscuits and Kelly. Ask the children to retell the key events in the chapter, and make notes of the sequence of events on the board. Discuss how the tone used to describe the events might be different if it were told from another character's point of view – for example, ask the children to suggest how Jake might have described Tim's attempt at abseiling.

● Arrange the children into groups of four.

Allocate a main character to each child and give them a character name card. Beginning with the first key event written on the board, ask the first character (for example, Jake) to describe the event using the first-person voice. Move the retelling around the group, asking the second character to describe the second event and so on until everything that happened in the chapter has been described from different characters' points of view.

● Ask the children to compare how the events appear differently when told, for example, by Giles.

> **Differentiation**
> **For older/more confident learners:** Ask the children to choose a different chapter and retell it from another character's point of view.
> **For younger/less confident learners:** Choose one character and ask children to take turns to describe the events from that character's point of view.

Plot, character and setting

Character traits

Objective: To identify key characteristics of the characters.
What you need: Copies of *Cliffhanger* and copies of photocopiable page 17.

What to do

● Ask the children to work with a partner, and give each child a copy of photocopiable page 17.
● Explain that character traits are qualities or characteristics that show a character's personality or what sort of person they are. Invite the children to read the list of character traits on the right of the page first, making sure they understand them. Then ask them to read the names of the characters on the left of the page. Can they say who Mrs Parsons is? Who can find her name in the story? (She is mentioned on the postcards.)
● Ask the children to discuss which character they think best fits each character trait before they begin, and then compare their ideas. Explain that one character may display more than one trait.
● Invite them to look through the book and find evidence that justifies their choice of character – for example, if they think Kelly fits *bubbly and full of energy*, they should find a page or section of the story that justifies this. (For example, her arrival at the Adventure Centre in Chapter One.) Encourage the children to skim through the story and find sentences to quote.
● Ask the pairs to compare their answers with another pair and discuss the reasons for their choices.

Differentiation
For older/more confident learners: Invite the children to find two or more sentences that justify their choices.
For younger/less confident learners: Instead of quoting directly from the text, allow children to use their own words to support their choice – for example, *Giles thinks he is good at everything.*

What happened when…?

Objective: To make notes and use evidence from across a text to explain events.
What you need: Copies of *Cliffhanger*, copies of photocopiable page 18 and scissors.

What to do

● Ask the children to do this activity after they have read the whole story. Explain that recognising and understanding cause and effect helps them to understand why characters behave in certain ways and how their actions affect the events in a story. The actions a character takes in response to an event can also help readers to understand a character's personality.
● Tell the children to work with a partner. Ask the pairs to look through the book, find some of the key events that occurred and think about what happened next. Each child should take it in turns to find an event in the story and ask their partner: *What happened when…?* The other child answers from memory, then they swap roles.
● Provide a copy of photocopiable page 18 for each child. Ask them to work individually to complete the sentences.
● Choose some of the children to read their completed sentences to the rest of the group.

Differentiation
For older/more confident learners: Ask children to cut out each sentence, mix them up, and then re-order them into the correct sequence.
For younger/less confident learners: Allow the children to refer to the story to help them to finish the sentences.

Plot, character and setting

The Crazy Bucket race

Objective: To write a story map.
What you need: Copies of *Cliffhanger*, large sheets of paper and pens.
Cross-curricular links: Art and design, geography.

What to do

● Try this activity when the children have read Chapter Five. During a shared writing session, invite the children to describe the features that were part of the obstacle race. (The paddling pool, full buckets of water, a run round the field, the slide, the sandpit, the stream, drainpipes.) Write the list of obstacles on the board.
● Ask the children to describe, from memory, what the characters had to do in the race.
● Encourage the children to close their eyes, then read out the paragraph that explains the race and ask them to picture it in their mind's eye.
● Explain that they are going to draw story maps of the obstacle race on large sheets of paper. They are then going to draw and/or write what happens to each character at each key point in the race. Tell them to allocate a different colour to each character and draw a line on the story map to show the character's progress through the course. Briefly go through the events of the race orally and allow the children to scan the text to check what happens as they draw their maps. Encourage them to add detail, such as *Tim fell here, Kelly knocked a Cheetah over here*.

Differentiation
For older/more confident learners: Ask children to draw their story map from memory first, and then to check it against the text.
For younger/less confident learners: Organise the children into small groups, and allocate a character to each member of the group. Let them take turns to add their character to the group's map.

Key moments

Objective: To retell the main points of the story in sequence.
What you need: Copies of *Cliffhanger*, paper, scissors and glue.

What to do

● Plan this activity for two separate occasions. Explain to the class that the key events are events without which the plot would be different or might not make sense. Encourage the children to suggest some events from the story, from memory, that could be omitted without affecting the plot or sense of the story. (Answers might include Kelly and Tim going into the wrong rooms, Giles banging Tim with the tennis racquet, details of what Biscuits eats.) Ask the children to work with a partner to skim through each chapter and discuss what they think are the key events in each.
● On the second occasion, ask the children to draw up a list of key events from the story from memory, in sequence. Tell them not to show them to their partner.
● Provide the children with scissors and ask them to cut out and mix up the key events before swapping them with their partner. Give each child another sheet of paper and glue, and invite them to read their partner's cut-out key events. They should arrange them into the correct sequence before gluing them onto the sheet of paper. Tell them to swap again with their partner, who can then check that the events are reassembled in the correct sequence.

Differentiation
For older/more confident learners: Ask pairs of children to read each other's list of key events and make connections about cause and effect that link these events in the story.
For younger/less confident learners: Make notes from the first part of this activity and let children refer to these.

Scary moments

● In each section of the timeline, describe how you feel when you have to do an activity that scares you.

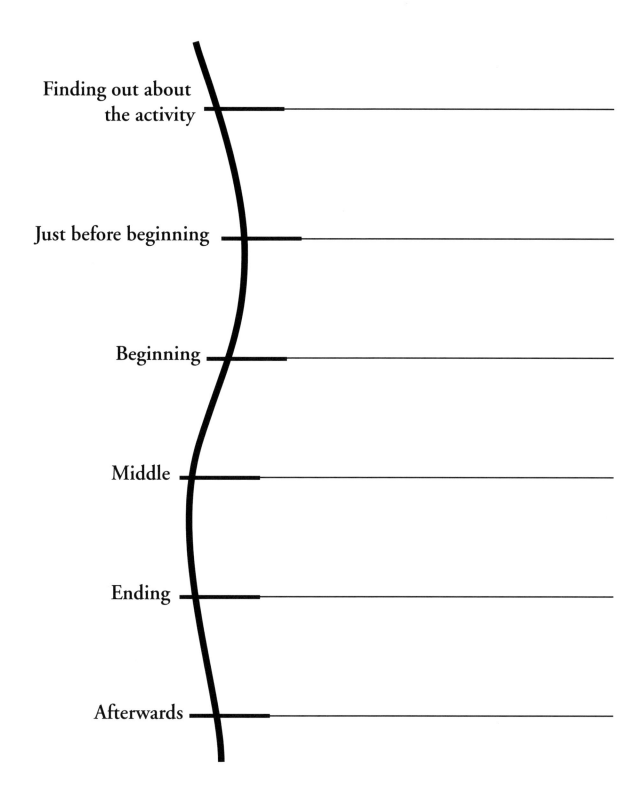

Finding out about
the activity

Just before beginning

Beginning

Middle

Ending

Afterwards

SECTION
4

Biscuits

● In the box beside each sentence from the story, write a word to describe Biscuits.

'Less of the Fatso, Piles,' he said, munching.	
He quietly passed me a tissue.	
'I do sumo wrestling, right?' he said, beating his chest. 'So you'd better watch your step, Piles.'	
Biscuits suddenly stepped forward. 'I'll have a go,' he said.	
Biscuits emptied the Frosties all over him.	
'Maybe you'd better go and get them bandaged?' said Biscuits.	

READ & RESPOND: Activities based on Cliffhanger

Illustration © 1995, Nick Sharratt

SCHOLASTIC
www.scholastic.co.uk

Character traits

● Match the characters to the character traits. (Each character may display more than one trait.)

Tim

Giles

Jake

Mrs Parsons

Kelly

Biscuits

bubbly and full of energy

loyal to friends

clever

arrogant and always wants to win

noisy

thoughtful

timid

over-protective

Plot, character and setting

What happened when...?

● Think carefully about what happens in *Cliffhanger* and complete these sentences.

When Kelly asked Sally about abseiling,

When Tim said he was OK at maths,

When Tim was teased after the game of Triangles,

When Giles demonstrated judo on Tim,

When Biscuits volunteered to go first at abseiling,

When Tim let go of the rope,

When Tim collected some balls with Jake,

When Kelly dropped Theresa in the river,

When one of the Cheetahs bumped into Tim,

When Tim worked out how to fill the baby big cat bins,

READ & RESPOND: Activities based on *Cliffhanger*

Illustration © 1995, Nick Sharratt

■SCHOLASTIC
www.scholastic.co.uk

Talk about it

Tim persuades Dad

Objective: To empathise with a character.
What you need: Copies of *Cliffhanger*.

What to do
● Use this activity when the children have read the first chapter.
● Read the opening paragraph. Point out that Tim says, *I kept telling and telling Dad*. Ask the children to skim the chapter and see if they can find anything that Tim tells his dad. Ask: *How does Tim respond when his dad encourages him to go on the holiday?* (He doesn't say anything but keeps looking at the television.)
● Ask the children to work in groups and discuss what Tim could have said to his dad to change his mind and not send Tim on the holiday. After a few minutes, arrange the children into pairs and allocate one to be Tim and the other to be Dad. Ask the pairs to hold a conversation where

Dad tries to persuade Tim that he will enjoy the holiday, and Tim tries to convince Dad that he will hate it. Explain that they should listen to each other's points and answer them, rather than just having an argument.
● Invite some of the pairs to role play their dialogues for the other children. Ask the watching children to say which side of the conversation was the most persuasive and why.

Differentiation
For older/more confident learners: Ask children to give a short talk on why Tim *should* go on the holiday and then on why Tim *should not* go.
For younger/less confident learners: Provide prompts and suggestions written on slips of paper that will help them to think of points for both sides of the argument. For example, *You will make new friends; I will feel too homesick; You need some healthy exercise; I'd prefer to read a book instead of running about.*

Feelings

Objective: To discuss characters' feelings.
What you need: Copies of *Cliffhanger* and copies of photocopiable page 22.
Cross-curricular link: PSHE.

What to do
● Use this activity when the children have finished the book.
● Discuss the range of feelings experienced by Tim in the story. Initially, allow the children to refer to the book to help them, and encourage them to infer Tim's feelings from the postcards. Then challenge them to think of feelings experienced by other characters at different points in the story – for example, how did Kelly feel when she dropped her troll doll in the river? How did Giles feel when the Tigers lost?
● Organise the children into pairs. Provide each pair with a copy of photocopiable page 22. Encourage the children to list in the thought

bubbles on the sheet the various feelings the characters experienced. Ask the pairs to discuss their ideas as they work.
● Then, in the centre column, the children can list the characters who might have experienced the feelings. Encourage them to discuss when and why the characters had these feelings. Ask them to draw a line to link the feelings to each character.
● Invite the children to count which characters experienced the most feelings and which feeling was the one most experienced in the story.

Differentiation
For older/more confident learners: Encourage children to find alternative words to describe feelings by using a thesaurus. Add more feelings bubbles to the photocopiable sheet.
For younger/less confident learners: Let children refer to the book to identify which characters experienced different feelings.

Talk about it

Giles in the hot-seat

> **Objective:** To understand how a character develops during a story.
> **What you need:** Copies of *Cliffhanger* and copies of the cards from photocopiable page 23.

What to do

● It might be useful to do this activity after the children have completed the 'Viewpoint' activity on page 12.

● Ask the children to think about the characters of Tim and Giles. Invite them to describe how each of them acts and feels at the start of the story. Encourage the children to say why they think Giles was unpleasant to Tim.

● Invite them to flick through the book to find any occasions when Giles acted in a more friendly way. (Pretending to be a Panther and joining in the gorilla impersonations in Chapter Two, and celebrating winning the race in Chapter Five.)

● Encourage the children to describe Giles'

behaviour to the other characters in the story and elicit that he was generally unpleasant to everyone. Invite them to describe how Giles reacted when Tim solved the puzzle of the obstacle race.

● Invite the children to take turns to sit in the hot-seat in the role of Giles and to describe his experience of the adventure holiday in the sequence of the story. Provide the other children with the question starter cards from photocopiable page 23. Encourage them to ask 'Giles' questions to enhance and deepen his responses.

> **Differentiation**
> **For older/more confident learners:** Invite children to write some questions of their own to ask Giles instead of using the question starter cards.
> **For younger/less confident learners:** Before the hot-seat session, allow the children time to think of a question to ask and write it onto the card.

Is it all right to be scared?

> **Objective:** To explore feelings.
> **What you need:** Copies of *Cliffhanger*.
> **Cross-curricular link:** PSHE.

What to do

● Try this activity when the children have read Chapter Three. It might be useful to do it after the children have completed the 'Scary moments' activity on page 11.

● Discuss how Tim feels about abseiling and ask the children to say why they think he is so scared. Encourage the children to describe any occasions when they have felt scared and to explain why.

● Draw up a list of reasons for feeling scared. Some of the responses might include: fear of getting hurt; fear of looking silly in front of others; fear of getting into trouble; fear of something unknown.

● Invite the children to suggest occasions when it

is good to be scared of something – for example, in a dangerous situation – and when it is silly to be scared – for example, when it stops a person from doing something they would like to do.

● Encourage the children to talk about how they can overcome feelings of fear. Do they do anything to help them cope, such as crossing their fingers, taking deep breaths or talking to someone about it? Discuss irrational fears that people have, such as fear of the dark or fear of spiders, and ways to overcome these.

> **Differentiation**
> **For older/more confident learners:** These children should be able to talk about fear as an idea, and understand when fear is helpful and when it is irrational.
> **For younger/less confident learners:** These children tend to relate fear to themselves, rather than thinking about it as an idea.

Talk about it

Freeze-frame

Objective: To explore scenes from the story.
What you need: Copies of *Cliffhanger*.

What to do

● Explain to the children that they are going to 'pause the story' as if they were pausing a film and create a freeze-frame moment. Choose a moment from the story in order to demonstrate how this is done – for example, when the group of children are having tea on the first night. Discuss what each character might be thinking at this moment.

● Organise the class into small groups of different numbers of children so there are groups of five, four, three and a pair. This means that they will be able to choose different scenes from across the book.

● Ask the children to look through the book and choose a scene from the story that suits the number of members of their group. Ask them to allocate a character to each child in the group and collaborate to work out and write down how the scene might look.

● Invite each group to show their chosen scene as a freeze-frame, one by one. Encourage each child in the scene to describe what they are thinking at that moment and to say what they will do next.

Differentiation
For older/more confident learners: Ask children to write a description of the scene that was chosen and enacted by their group.
For younger/less confident learners: Encourage children to draw a picture of their group's freeze-frame moment.

Meeting up again

Objective: To act out a new event.
What you need: Copies of *Cliffhanger*, copies of photocopiable page 24, scissors, glue sticks or straws, coloured pens and a digital video recorder and player.

What to do

● Read out the two postcards at the end of the story. Explain to the children that you want them to imagine a new scene when Tim, Kelly and Biscuits meet again after the adventure holiday. Discuss a setting for the new scene. It might be at Tim's house, on a new adventure holiday, or in a café, for example.

● Arrange the children into groups of three or four and suggest that they include Giles in the new scene. Allow the groups sufficient time to discuss and agree on the setting, what happens, dialogue and the allocation of characters. Stress that the children should work closely together,

listening to and responding to each other's ideas.

● Hand out copies of photocopiable page 24 to groups. Ask the children to cut out the characters and glue them onto sticks or straws to make stick puppets. They may want to colour them in first.

● Encourage the groups to rehearse their new scenes. When they are happy with them, they can perform their new scenes with the puppets. You could record the performances and play them back to the class. Compare the children's ideas. How similar or different are they?

Differentiation
For older/more confident learners: Encourage children to write up their new scenes as a playscript.
For younger/less confident learners: These children might need help to cut out the characters. Encourage them to recreate a scene from the story rather than create a new scene.

Feelings

● Write in the thought bubbles all the 'feelings' from the story you can think of. In the centre, write the names of the characters who experienced the feelings and draw a line to link the character to the feeling. The first one has been done for you.

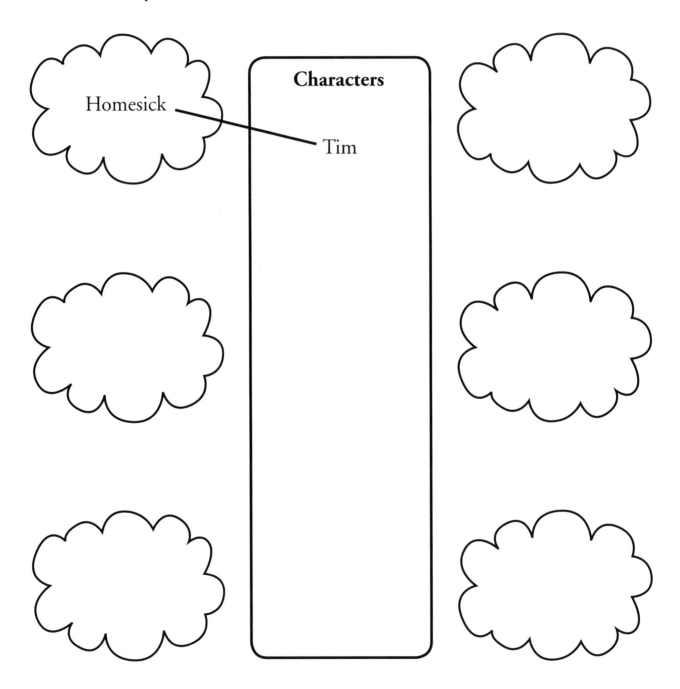

Characters

Homesick

Tim

Giles in the hot-seat

● Use these cards to help you plan questions to ask Giles.

✂

What was your first impression of...	Why did you...
Why didn't you...	When were you most...
What did you enjoy about...	Who would you like to...
What did you do when Tim...	What did you think when Kelly...
What was the best thing about...	What was the worst thing about...
What would you do differently...	At the end, how did you feel about...

Meeting up again

● Cut out the characters and glue them on to sticks or straws to make puppets for your new story scenes.

Illustrations © 1995, Nick Sharratt

Dear Dad

Objective: To write a persuasive letter.
What you need: Copies of *Cliffhanger*, whiteboard or flipchart and pens.

What to do
● Try this activity when the children have read Chapter One.
● Explain to the children that they are going to write a letter from Tim to his dad to try to persuade him that the adventure holiday is a bad idea before he is sent on the trip. Recap the layout and features of letter writing and discuss the 'audience' for the letter – Tim's dad. Ask the children to suggest the tone of language for the letter. As Tim knows his dad well, should it be formal or informal? Ask the children to read Tim's first postcard as an example of the tone Tim uses. Discuss the purpose of the letter – to persuade. Work with the children to write several sentences that could be used – for example:

> *Dear Dad,*
> *I really, really think this holiday is a very BAD idea and so will you when you read this letter!*

● Use shared writing to expand the ideas and add Tim's main reasons for strongly disliking the idea of the holiday. Encourage the children to use quite extravagant vocabulary to describe what could go wrong for Tim on the trip.
● Now invite the children to write their letter.
● Hold a plenary session to share some of their finished letters.

Differentiation
For older/more confident learners: Encourage children to edit their letters on a computer.
For younger/less confident learners: Work with children in a group to help them to use the first person consistently.

Come to the Adventure Centre!

Objective: To create a persuasive advertisement.
What you need: Copies of *Cliffhanger*, whiteboard or flipchart, photocopiable page 28, writing and drawing materials.

What to do
● This activity will work best when the children have finished reading the story.
● Ask the children if they can remember how Tim's dad found out about the adventure holiday. Read the second paragraph of Chapter One aloud. Explain to the children that they are going to create the newspaper advertisement for the adventure holiday.
● Discuss the purpose of the advert – to make readers want to go on the holiday. Use shared writing to collect some ideas. Invite the children to suggest reasons why someone would want to go on this holiday. Draw up a list of activities the children think should take place. What else would they enjoy apart from the activities? Draw up a list of adjectives they could use to describe the centre and the activities. Talk about how rhetorical questions are often used in advertisements and add one or two to the board, such as: *Are you a couch potato?* or *Will you take the challenge?*
● Ask the children to work in small groups or in pairs and provide them with the prompts on photocopiable page 28. Ask them to share their ideas and write them onto the prompt sheet. They can then create their adverts individually.

Differentiation
For older/more confident learners: Ask children to use a computer to create their adverts using different font effects and clip art to enhance them.
For younger/less confident learners: Let children continue writing the advert in small groups or with a partner, rather than individually.

Get writing

Holiday diary

> **Objective:** To write from another character's point of view.
> **What you need:** Copies of *Cliffhanger* and copies of photocopiable page 29.

What to do

● Invite the children to do this activity after they have read the whole book. It would also be beneficial to complete this activity when the children have done the 'Feelings' activity from page 19 and the 'Viewpoint' activity from page 12 of this book.

● Invite the children to read the beginning of Chapter Six and find out how long the activity holiday lasted. (Four days.)

● Ask the children to summarise the events of each day from Tim's point of view, then from Biscuits', Giles' and Kelly's points of view. Encourage them to describe how Biscuits' feelings about the holiday might be different from Tim's. Repeat with the other two characters.

● Explain that they are to choose Biscuits, Giles or Kelly and write a diary for the holiday from their chosen character's point of view. Discuss the style of language used in a diary (informal) and the audience (the diary writer). Remind the children to use the first-person voice.

● Provide the children with copies of photocopiable page 29 to help them recall the order of events so they can focus on the feelings of their character.

> **Differentiation**
> **For older/more confident learners:** Children can write their diary without using the photocopiable sheet.
> **For younger/less confident learners:** Work with these children as a group and discuss ideas as they write. You could ask them to write the diary from Tim's point of view only.

Race commentary

> **Objective:** To write a radio commentary.
> **What you need:** Copies of *Cliffhanger*, audio recorder and a recording of a sports commentary (optional).
> **Cross-curricular link:** ICT.

What to do

● You can complete this activity after the children have created story maps in the activity 'The Crazy Bucket race' on page 14 of this book.

● Talk to the children about any events they have seen on television or listened to on the radio that feature a sports commentary. Discuss the purpose of commentaries and explain that the commentator needs to convey what is happening as accurately as possible, because the audience is not there. If possible, play a football or tennis radio commentary to the children.

● Explain to the children that they are going to use their story maps for the Crazy Bucket race to write a radio commentary. Hold a shared writing session and discuss the purpose (conveying details about an event) and audience (listeners). Talk about the language to use – for example, they should address the listener personally and use present-tense verbs. Model a few sentences to begin the commentary. For example: *Welcome to the Crazy Bucket race! We have four teams of youngsters ready to battle it out to give the baby big cats the most water in the shortest time. I can just hear Sally getting them ready... and they're off!*

● Invite the children to write their race commentaries with a partner and then to record them, taking turns to read a section each.

● Play some of their commentaries in a plenary.

> **Differentiation**
> **For older/more confident learners:** Let children write their commentaries individually.
> **For younger/less confident learners:** Children can work as a group to write the commentary using the group story map.

Get writing

Postcards home

> **Objective:** To write from another character's point of view.
> **What you need:** Copies of *Cliffhanger*, and plain postcards or postcard-sized pieces of paper.

What to do
- Complete this activity when the children have finished reading the story.
- Tell the children to read just the postcards from the book. Ask them to say what they notice about how the postcards show Tim's changing feelings during the holiday.
- Discuss the purpose of postcards (to give brief information, usually about a holiday) and the audience (friends and family). Ask the children to describe the tone and style of language used in writing postcards. (Informal and brief.)
- Explain that they are going to write three postcards from a different character's viewpoint – either Giles or Biscuits. The first postcard should be from the first day when they arrived at the Adventure Centre, the second from the middle of the holiday and the third from the last day.
- Encourage the children to suggest what sort of things Giles would focus on, such as how useless Tim and Biscuits are and how good he is at all the activities; and the things Biscuits would focus on, such as needing more food and his friendship with Tim.
- Provide the children with three postcards or postcard-sized pieces of paper and ask them to choose to be either Giles or Biscuits and write their postcards home.

> **Differentiation**
> **For older/more confident learners:** Encourage children to write another postcard from Biscuits or Kelly in reply to Tim's postcards at the end of the book.
> **For younger/less confident learners:** Work with small groups and ask them to rehearse their postcards orally before writing.

Meeting up once more

> **Objective:** To write dialogue as a playscript.
> **What you need:** Copies of *Cliffhanger*, copies of photocopiable page 30, board or flipchart and children's recorded role plays from 'Meeting up again', page 21.

What to do
- This activity follows on from the 'Meeting up again' activity on page 21. Ask the children to work in the same groups they were in when they created a role play of a new scene. Explain that they are now going to write their role plays as playscripts for performance.
- Using one of the recorded role plays, encourage the children to contribute to writing it on the board in a shared writing session.
- Before they begin to write, discuss the conventions for setting out a playscript, including the cast list and stage directions. Let the children watch their group's role-play recording before they begin writing.
- Provide them with the script-writing template from photocopiable page 30 and ask them to write their playscripts individually, continuing on another sheet.
- Hold a plenary session and invite the children to have a group reading of their plays. Encourage them to describe the differences between their written plays and their role-play versions. Was it easier to read their scripts or to do the role play? Have they improved their original role plays?

> **Differentiation**
> **For older/more confident learners:** Encourage children to lay out their playscripts correctly on a computer.
> **For younger/less confident learners:** Support children work in their groups, each writing their own character's part.

Come to the Adventure Centre!

● Use this sheet to plan your advert.

Write an eye-catching title for the advert here:
Where is the centre? What is good about the place?
What sort of children would enjoy this holiday? What ages should they be?
What activities are there?
What are the rooms and meals like?
What other people will they meet?
How much will it cost?
Ask the readers a question.

Holiday diary

● Choose a character and write their diary entries on these pages.

Day 1
Arriving:

Tea:

After tea:

Bedtime:

Day 2
Going abseiling:

Day 3
Canoeing:

After tea:

Day 4
The Crazy Bucket race:

The Camp Cook-Out:

Meeting up once more

Title:

Cast list:

Describe the scene (inside brackets):

The name of the character each time they speak; how they speak and any actions they make (inside brackets)	Spoken words	Stage directions describing actions they make after speaking (inside brackets)

Assessment

Assessment advice

Cliffhanger is a fast-paced adventure story written about a boy who is sent on an activity holiday. The activities terrify him and they are not the sort of adventures he wants to have. The main theme is that of a boy who, albeit reluctantly, faces up to his fears and comes out on top, showing children that everyone has different talents and abilities that are worth being proud of.

Jacqueline Wilson writes with a great deal of humour as she deals with Tim's underlying problems. Readers should be able to empathise with Tim's fears, his clumsiness and lack of self-esteem and courage.

This provides an ideal opportunity for assessing children's ability to read beyond the events and between the lines to discover motives behind characters' behaviour.

Ask the children questions as they read about how characters feel at certain points – for example, *When Tim writes his first postcard how is he feeling? What happens to affect how he feels?* Encourage them to support their suggestions with reasons – for example, by asking: *What is there in the text that makes you think that?*

Humour is another of the important elements in the story. Invite the children to identify any actions, events or dialogue they thought was funny and to say why. How would the story change if it were not told with humour?

When the children do the assessment activity, their answers to the questions will demonstrate their ability to empathise with characters and to think beyond the obvious simple responses.

How did Tim feel?

> **Assessment focus:** To demonstrate an ability to read between the lines of a text and empathise with a character's feelings; to sequence events.
> **What you need:** Copies of *Cliffhanger*, copies of photocopiable page 32, scissors and coloured pens.

What to do
● Remind the children of the work they have done as they have read *Cliffhanger* on investigating viewpoint and characters' feelings. Provide them with a copy of photocopiable page 32, coloured pens and scissors.
● Ask the children, working individually, to read the list of questions and write out their answers in the spaces provided on the sheet. They can then cut out the strips and put the events into the order in which they occur in the story.
● Once the children have ordered the questions, ask them to read through each one again and find the relevant section in the story. Invite them to check with the story and to add to or alter their original response if they wish to improve it, using a different-coloured pen. Explain that they can make notes on the reverse of key points as they check with the story to help them to give their answers. Encourage them to write more than one sentence.
● Next, invite the children to give their answers orally, and then to choose the question where they think they have given the best final answer. Ask them to copy out this question onto a sheet of paper and to write their answer in full underneath.

How did Tim feel?

● Answer the questions then cut them out and put them into the sequence of the story. Check your answers with the story and add anything that will improve them using a different-coloured pen.

How did Tim feel when he showed Giles his safety helmet?

Why did he feel like that?

How did Tim feel when he, Giles and Biscuits stayed up swapping jokes?

Why did he feel like that?

How did Tim feel when he shouted, 'No, *you* shut up Giles'?

Why did he feel like that?

How did Tim feel when he saw Walter Bear on the back seat of the car?

Why did he feel like that?

How did Tim feel when his dad suggested an adventure holiday?

Why did he feel like that?

How did Tim feel when he had finished abseiling?

Why did he feel like that?

Illustration © 1995, Nick Sharratt